Secret Shame

SECRET
shame

OVERCOMING PAIN AND BROKENNESS
AFTER AN ABORTION

Angel L. Murchison

NEW YORK

LONDON • NASHVILLE • MELBOURNE • VANCOUVER

SECRET shame
OVERCOMING PAIN AND BROKENNESS AFTER AN ABORTION

Published in New York, New York, by Morgan James Publishing. Morgan James is a trademark of Morgan James, LLC. www.MorganJamesPublishing.com

Scripture taken from the New King James Version®. Copyright © 1982 by Thomas Nelson. Used by permission. All rights reserved.

Proudly distributed by Ingram Publisher Services.

Morgan James BOGO™

A **FREE** ebook edition is available for you or a friend with the purchase of this print book.

CLEARLY SIGN YOUR NAME ABOVE

Instructions to claim your free ebook edition:
1. Visit MorganJamesBOGO.com
2. Sign your name CLEARLY in the space above
3. Complete the form and submit a photo of this entire page
4. You or your friend can download the ebook to your preferred device

ISBN 9781631958991 paperback
ISBN 9781631959004 ebook
Library of Congress Control Number: 2022932035

Cover Design by:
Rachel Lopez
www.r2cdesign.com

Interior Design by:
Chris Treccani
www.3dogcreative.net

Morgan James PUBLISHING

Builds with... **Habitat for Humanity®** Peninsula and Greater Williamsburg

Morgan James is a proud partner of Habitat for Humanity Peninsula and Greater Williamsburg. Partners in building since 2006.

Get involved today! Visit MorganJamesPublishing.com/giving-back

I dedicate this book to my aborted son, Jeremiah Isaac Murchison. You have not been forgotten. Your life ended way too early, and I am so very sorry. I look forward to meeting you someday on the other side, my son.

I believe Jesus gave me that name for you. You were a very special child. You went to heaven early in your life, and for that I am so very sorry. In the Bible, we read the account of how Abraham was going to sacrifice Isaac, but Jesus provided the sacrifice.

I sacrificed your life, Jeremiah Isaac; I made the wrong choice. I pray God uses that choice to help other women in any way He can. Maybe it will help another woman choose not to take her child's life. I'm sorry it cost you your life here on earth, Jeremiah. You are with Jesus now, and He's the best parent a child could ever have.

Jeremiah, Mommy loves you, and Mommy misses you. I wish I could remember when you went to heaven. I know it was not winter; it seems it may have been summer when there went a baby unborn, leaving emptiness inside only Jesus could heal.

Love is not a feeling; love is not sex. Love is knowing You, oh Lord. Oh, what a blessing, knowing You, Lord.

Table Of Contents

ACKNOWLEDGMENTS

It has been twenty-seven years since the Creator of the Universe, my Creator, spoke to me about writing a book. I now have put the final words to a book that was the hardest book, the most difficult assignment God has ever given me. I have completed many tasks and have done a lot at God's request, but nothing that took this long and with so many tears and some laughter on a roller coaster ride of my emotions. This book I believe will one day soon become a movie.

I love to write; I love to help people, and I love to share my faith. I would do anything for Jesus. This assignment from him is now complete. The final chapter of this book, the hardest writing I have ever penned or maybe will ever write is now done, twenty-seven years after his first request.

Although I write daily and my devotion and words to God in my *Good Morning Beautiful People* series will continue, I can't express how blessed I am to finally put the final touches on a book that was a request to me from God Himself. It certainly was a long-term assignment and the most difficult assignment I have ever received.

Many thanks to my family and friends for journeying with me. I love you all.

To W. Terry Whalin, thank you for the invitation to Author University 101 in Los Angeles, California. Your contract offer helped me believe God did indeed call me to write and share my story with the world. Several contracts later with your patience, prayers, and understanding, I now have made it to completion.

To the Morgan James Publishing family, thank you for believing in the book and helping me navigate the message I wanted to share with the world. You are all amazing people.

For my editor, Aubrey Kosa, thank you for helping me untangle my words. I will be forever grateful.

To my aborted son, Jeremiah, I told you so my precious child. I told you that God would open doors for me to speak about the pain and trauma of abortion. Women will be set free. I miss you still; I miss you much. I know you are with Jesus, and I'll see you again someday. Oh, Jeremiah, how I love you! You are the only child I have who likes to hear "I told you so."

To the many millions of women who are suffering the aftermath of an abortion, I know your pain; I felt the shame. The time has come now for you to heal.

Introduction

My Father's Love

~~~~~~

Oh, Father, Your love for me is so hard to comprehend.
You died for me when I was yet a sinner.

Love, you had no boundaries. You took my sin, and
You made me whole again.
Such love, the love of my Father.
When I chose the path of the evil one, You loved me
and led me to Your path again.
Such love, the love of my Father.

When I cried because of all the pain, You healed the
pain and removed my shame.
Oh, such love.
Where others wounded me, You bound up my
wounds and filled me with joy.

Such love, the love of my Father.

When I needed guidance, You left me your Word
and your Holy Spirit.
Such love, the love of my Father.
Whatever the future holds for me is in Your hands,
for Your love for me has made me whole.
My Father, You say in Your Word that the footsteps
of the righteous are ordered of the Lord.
This is my future, because of the love of my Father.

~~~~~~~~~~~~~~~~~~~~~~~~~~~~~~~~~~~~~~

The Holy Spirit inspired me to write that poem
during my lunch one very cold, winter day, and it was
the catalyst for penning this memoir. It was not only the
Holy Spirit that prompted me to share His living words
and embody the healing balm of Gilead for a broken
and hurting world but also revelations from the Word of
God. Bible passages like Psalm 139 tugged at my heart,
urging me to write my story. Verse after verse con-
firmed that God formed me. He knew me in my mother's womb, and I was fearfully and wonderfully made.
Despite the title of this memoir, shame has no place in
God's world—or in my thinking. He destined me to be
His handmaiden. He made me His hands and His feet so
that I could pen my journey of shame—the pain I would
hide—and shine a light in a dark world.

My prayer is that my story will touch your heart and you too will be set free. Every life has a plan, and God's heart yearns for each of us to fulfill it.

> *"For I know the thoughts that I think toward you," says the Lord, "thoughts of peace and not of evil, to give you a future and a hope."*
> —Jeremiah 29:11

I feel truly blessed that you are reading my life story. I hope it touches you and inspires you to step out and fulfill the purpose He created for you. You have a specific destiny only you can fulfill.

> *For You formed my inward parts; You covered me in my mother's womb. I will praise You, for I am fearfully and wonderfully made; Marvelous are Your works, And that my soul knows very well. My frame was not hidden from You, When I was made in secret, And skillfully wrought in the lowest parts of the earth. Your eyes saw my substance, being yet unformed. And in Your book they all were written, The days fashioned for me, When as yet there were none of them.* —Psalm 139:13–16

CHAPTER ONE

A Martini While You Wait?

July 15, 1962, in Fort Kent, Maine, was the day God breathed life into me. That is the day my journey of life began.

I was the fourteenth birth for my parents. Born into an impoverished family, being the fourteenth child was my introduction to shame. As an intense combination of feelings, shame can be very difficult to identify, but looking back, it was shame that caused me great angst as a child. I didn't really feel wanted. Fourteen children in one family is a lot, especially in today's world, and I remember asking God if I was a wanted child. His reply was a resounding *yes*, and through his Word, I began my journey of believing God.

I learned that He had a plan for me before the foundations of the earth were set, and I began to believe in that plan and asked Him to bring it to fruition. I wanted to know His plan—the reason I was created, my purpose, and my destiny were before me—and I began to talk with Him about it through prayer.

I wanted to walk in His plan and bring it to life. I wanted to know why I was born. I asked Him many questions day and night, begging Him to fulfill his plan. When I knew I had blown my plans, my dreams and I needed a new path—God's plan. I would pray, "Please, God, take my mess and bring a great message." I prayed to a loving God—a Heavenly Father who had a purpose, a plan for the poor girl, the girl raised on the wrong side of the tracks. That was me, and I wanted to journey on—God's way.

I still like to tease my brothers and sisters, telling them that God saved the best for last. My position in the family as the youngest child is a bit challenging (although I'd be willing to bet any position in a family of fourteen is a bit challenging). One of my sisters has no problem telling me that life was much better before I came along. I stole her thunder. I always reply, "Sorry, sis, you will just have to take it up with Jesus. I am walking out my destiny and the purpose for my life. He has a great plan for you, as well." We joke this way often.

When I was five years old and ready to attend kindergarten, one of my sisters would walk me, holding my hand, to school in the mornings. This is my first memory of my childhood—a childhood that would be filled with pain, yet I was a child of destiny. One sister named me Lavina Gail, and another sister named me Angel. Angel stuck. Later, my name was officially changed to Angel Lavina.

I still don't know what my mother wanted to name me.

When I was in second grade, my mother died. After she died, my life consisted of living with a dad who struggled with alcohol, a developmentally delayed sister, a crippled sister (she had a rare bone disease), and a whole lot of other brothers and sisters. When you are the youngest in the family, everyone is the boss except you.

I never mourned my mother's death with the rest of my family. Consequently, I had no closure on the loss of my mother until many years later. This kept me bound in those shackles until Jesus Christ healed that part of my life. Losing a mother is a great loss to any young child. Thank you, Jesus, for healing me and filling my mother's void in my life. She was a gem, and I am thankful she gave me life.

Although I don't have too many memories of my childhood, I do remember being teased for where I lived. The other kids would make fun of the fact that I grew up on the wrong side of the tracks. I knew we were poor; I didn't need anyone to tell me.

Both kids and adults can be so cruel. The expression "sticks and stones may break my bones, but words will never hurt me" is completely false. The teasing words from my childhood remained seared on my mind and etched on my heart for decades until Jesus Christ Himself took the sting away. Those memories, although limited, reveal a young girl shrouded in shame and pain.

I began to drink as soon as I was able to get alcohol from my father or his girlfriend. I remember there was one Friday night in junior high school when I drank a Pepsi bottle filled with gin. I guess that was when I started looking for ways to medicate my pain. I didn't know about mixing alcohol; I just drank it straight from the bottle. That Sunday, over a day later, I finally woke up after consuming the bottle of straight gin. I should have died from alcohol poisoning that weekend, but God did not allow it. When I woke up, I remember my sister asking me if I wanted something to eat, and I responded that I wanted something like thirteen pancakes (some enormous amount). She inquired teasingly, "Do you want a martini while you wait?"

My attempts to hide my pain with alcohol were only temporary. One day, the Holy Spirit would gently guide me to face my fears and deal with all the shame and pain that had taken root in my life.

In the midst of this shame, pain, and drinking, I was attending church, and that church decided to start a school when I was in ninth grade. I desperately wanted to go. I loved the Lord, but I couldn't seem to walk with Him for very long periods of time. My dear sister paid for me to attend this school, an enormous sacrifice for her, as we were a very poor family. I attended that school for a year. Ironically, that Christian school was no different for me than the public setting I had left. I still didn't feel like I belonged. The church was splitting into many factions. This discord saddened me, and it just wasn't working out. I wanted out.

This division within the church and my resulting departure from their school only brought further confusion to an already dazed and confused young lady. I can remember asking the Lord, *Where is the love*? Now, I look back on both of those churches and the people involved and see that while I was a confused young girl, I loved them all.

Why didn't they love each other?

I have asked the Lord many times about the lack of love in His church, starting way back then. I was glad to leave the mess of the Christian school behind and move on with my life. I went back to attending a public school, quit church, and continued partying and living a destructive lifestyle. I couldn't identify with the Christian walk during that time, and it seemed easier to go back to the familiar. At least in my destructive lifestyle, I felt like I belonged.

I continued looking for love in all the wrong places, first with alcohol and then with a relationship that would turn out to change my life forever. I met a young man when I was fifteen, and we soon became sexually active. I remember thinking that there was finally someone to love me. I enjoyed being with him, and we spent every moment together. But I soon became pregnant. Not long after, the young man and I broke up. Although I believed I loved him, our relationship was toxic. It was destined to fail because of our codependency.

I told one of my family members about the pregnancy, and she arranged for another family member to take me downstate for an "office visit." She told me that many girls had the "procedure" done, and in a few minutes, it would all be over. She told me that the blob of tissue would be removed and that it wasn't a baby quite yet.

She was right about the speed. In a short time, it was over, but the pain of an abortion is a pain I wish I had never experienced. My life felt empty and cold, and I was embedded with a deeper shame than before.

I physically hurt. The cramping after the procedure is a cramping, I wish no human being would ever have to experience in their lifetime. I still remember the coldness of the room, the building that looked like a house. It was near a hospital in a city that seemed far, far away from home—the home that God chose for His daughter to live in, the red house on the wrong side of the tracks.

After the abortion appointment, my family member tried joking with me on the way home. For some reason, I did not feel much like laughing. Although I did not fully understand what had just taken place, I felt a great emptiness inside of me, another void, a feeling I cannot completely put into words. There was more pain for me to bury, more pain for me to hide.

I graduated from high school when I was just sixteen and moved to a larger city five hours away from my family. I went to hairdressing school, partied with mostly alcohol. I was doing everything I could to keep the pain locked in, looking for a better life. I worked part-time to pay my rent for an apartment that my niece and I leased. Other than the apartment, we did not have much. I was happy to have someone to help with expenses, and she and I became good friends during this time. She was much prettier than I, and the guys all seemed to like her better. She seemed to be more successful at hairdressing too. Although we both graduated from hairdressing school, she of course graduated first. She had never cut anyone's ear like I had (not a good day for the little old man in my chair when I gave his ear a slice, nor for me when I didn't know how to stop the bleeding).

During this time, I learned what it is like to go without the bare necessities. I remember trying to make some popcorn for breakfast early one morning not because we wanted too but because it was all we had. The pan caught fire because we had no cooking oil and, in frustration, I threw it out the window. Doing laundry was a luxury. When we couldn't afford to go to the laundromat, which was most of the time, we washed our clothes by hand each night. These were happy times, but hard times. Once a month, my brother would drive several hours to take us to the laundromat. We would wash everything that we could on those trips. He would bring us food, and those days, we thought we were in Heaven. He was, and still is today, an amazing brother with a heart of compassion like no other.

During this time, there was one night I became so intoxicated at a party that my friends literally dragged me home to my apartment. It was during the winter, and they forgot to put boots or any other shoes on my feet. I was freezing when we got back to my apartment, so they gave me a hot shower and put me to bed. I tried to get warm beneath the covers as my body continued to shake and shiver. My friends blow-dried my hair straight up in the air in an attempt to warm me up so that I looked like a troll. I had become quite ill, so they called the directors of the school I was attending, who came and took me to the local hospital. I had gotten frostbite from the cold. I was only seventeen years old and needed an adult signature before the hospital could treat me. My family was notified back home, and wow, they were not happy; however, they did give the hospital permission to treat me. I'm sure they were very concerned for me underneath their anger and annoyance, and they did the very best they could to help me. They were, and are, good people.

Soon, it was graduation day for hairdressing school, and I had to move back home. Things were different when I returned, but I am still not sure why. It is true that once you leave, you can't go home again. Things were not the same as when I left. I only worked one day as a hairdresser before I decided to leave for Connecticut to live with my brother and his family.

This short adventure with cosmetology highlights my lack of self-esteem. I was ashamed that it didn't work out.

I soon met some party buddies and spent most Saturdays at the beach. On Saturday nights, I could be found at bars all over Connecticut. Most Sundays, I was hungover. I remember being very ill one Sunday, and my dear brother took me to the hospital. I can still hear the doctor telling him, "She has very high alcohol content in her blood." I guess that was the only way I knew how to deal with the pain that kept consuming my life. I did not know any other way.

I worked two jobs and was able to buy a car with my brother's help, but nothing seemed to take the emptiness away. The guys I dated did not fill the void. My jobs did not fill the void. The partying did not fill the void. So, I consumed alcohol, and at least it made me feel happy—for a little while.

One weekend, a friend of mine graduated from college, and we went out to celebrate. I consumed too many mixed drinks that night but decided to drive home. I was on the wrong side of the road at one point and narrowly escaped a head-on collision. It terrified me.

Then I saw the blue lights behind me.

The police officer asked me if I had been drinking and demanded that I step out of my car. That really terrified me. He demanded I walk the center line of the road. By some miracle, he let me go and told me to drive straight home.

I can still see those blue lights in my mind just like it was yesterday. The Lord had spared my life, once again.

I sobered up quickly when I walked the center line in that pitch-black night. I could have taken someone else's life driving in that condition. I could have taken the lives of the people who were passengers with me or my own life, and I would have never forgiven myself for that.

Through the blur of partying while I lived in Connecticut, I still felt a connection to the boy I dated in high school. Even though we had been off and on in our relationship, I still had feelings for him. I finally got up the nerve to call him and told him that I would be back home to visit in a few months. I had called him many times in the previous eighteen months, but I would always just hang up before saying anything. I was tied to him in a way that I did not understand until much later in my life, something I now call a soul tie. We had gone too far in our physical relationship when we first dated, and even when we were not together, I still felt connected to him. That August, I visited him, and we talked about old times, fun times, hard times, and the future. We decided we wanted to marry and started making plans for a wedding that would take place the following August.

CHAPTER TWO

The Journey Begins

M y wedding day took place on August 5, 1985, at the Presque Isle Wesleyan Church. This was the church that my fiancé had attended.

My father walked me down the aisle that day, and I have often wondered what that was like for him. I knew my father loved me, even though he never told me. Alcohol kept his pain down most of his life. I don't know if he ever knew how to express love. He did the best he knew how, and for that, I am grateful.

We wore gray tuxedos paired with lavender and mauve Victorian gowns . . . I remember the day as if it was yesterday. I thought marriage would finally fill the void and bring me the happiness I so longed for, but it wasn't too long before I realized that my marriage was not going to be an easy road. My new husband was having difficulty finding steady work while I was enjoying my work at a local bank. He wanted to move back to Maine, so he went on ahead and found work at a hardware store a few hours away from our hometown. I soon followed, and we lived in a camper until it got too cold. Winter was quickly approaching. We then moved in with his parents back home. The expression goes "two women cannot live under the same roof," and this proved very true in this circumstance.

I was pregnant by then with my oldest daughter. I loved being pregnant. I loved eating cherry chocolates and the feeling of a child growing inside me. Being pregnant is one of the happiest memories of my life.

On May 15, 1985, weighing 9 pounds, 10 ounces, my oldest daughter entered our world. We were so proud of her, and she was most certainly the apple of our eyes. I loved to dress her in frilly dresses. Everyone admired her natural curls and big smile. Her father would bounce her, even when I warned him that she had just eaten. I laugh when I remember how she spit up in his mouth when he made her laugh too hard after she had just eaten.

Things were moving forward, and I thought maybe this would be the happiness I had so longed for.

Soon after our daughter was born, we bought our first home, a fixer-upper. I soon had to return to work full-time to help meet the expenses of fixing the home. My daughter stayed with her grandparents each day while I went to work. This is not what I wanted, but it was necessary during this time.

We had our daughter dedicated to the Lord, as I felt this was important. I don't know why I felt it was important since I was not serving the Lord at the time. I don't even remember having seen other children dedicated to the Lord; however, I knew our daughter was going to be.

I remember my father and my then-husband's grandfather coming to church with us on that special day—my daughter's baby dedication ceremony. As the two men put some money in the offering plate, my then-husband's grandfather said to my dad, "There goes our beer money for the day." They were both hard of hearing, so the whisper was more like a normal conversation level, and I knew many rows of parishioners heard them. I was embarrassed and felt a bit ashamed of their conversation, but I was glad they had come to celebrate my daughter's dedication to the Lord.

I intuitively knew that I wanted my daughter to know the Lord and live her life for Him, even though I had not yet committed *my* whole life to Him. Today I am thankful that I made the decision to dedicate her to the Lord and that she did grow up knowing Jesus. I know He is watching over her, and He has heard the many prayers prayed on her behalf.

Despite our new responsibilities as parents, my then-husband and I continued to party on weekends. We were both working and busy with our daughter, so weekends were the only time we had to party. Sometimes I would drive my daughter to Sunday school on Sunday mornings with a hangover. A few years ago, my daughter told me that she remembered when I would drink and drive with her when she was just a young child. I wish she did not have those memories, but she does, and they are a part of who she is and her testimony. And I know Jesus will redeem them and work them out according to His plan for her life.

My oldest daughter is a very gifted young woman. She is artistic and intelligent, and I know He has great plans for her life. I am excited for them to unfold. As I pen this book, she is married and a mother to three of the most handsome boys you will ever meet. Her life is full of work, school, hunting, fishing, and raising three boys. I like to tease her three sons by telling them their mother, their two aunts (my other daughters), and their grandmother are city girls compared to them.

Two years after the birth of my first daughter, I gave birth to another beautiful baby girl. I had many complications carrying her; my pregnancy was threatened from the very beginning. At one point, I was sent home to miscarry. I thank the Lord that this did not happen.

Around this same time, my sister was involved in a car accident in which her three-year-old son died. I dealt with so many emotions during this pregnancy, afraid of losing my baby, and this robbed me of my joy while carrying her.

Due to the complications I was having, I transferred from my doctor to a midwife in another town. She discovered what was causing the threat of this miscarriage and prescribed that I give birth using a new birthing chair. My then-husband would be the one to mostly deliver the baby and cut the umbilical cord with the midwife right there to assist in the delivery if needed.

The contractions started late one night. My then-husband thought maybe I could sleep it off and wait until the next morning; however, that was not what we had planned. We went to the hospital, and on the way, fear hit my husband. He decided that the midwife needed to earn her money by delivering the baby and cutting the umbilical cord. He wanted to be the one right beside us. My contractions stopped on our way to the hospital, and I remember faking them the rest of the way because I knew he had wanted to wait until morning. I was afraid he would be angry with me for insisting we go late at night.

Nonetheless, early the next morning, our second child entered the world. There were a few things they wanted to keep an eye on, but to me, she was perfect. Once again, I wanted to have my baby dedicated to the Lord. I still had not surrendered my life to Him fully; however, I prayed on occasion during my pregnancy as it was a difficult one. Then everything turned out fine, and I had another beautiful baby girl. She was a high-energy baby with personality plus. She liked to sleep during the day and stay awake at night. Despite her terrible sleeping pattern, she brought us such joy, and our family was certainly growing. I see the talent this young lady has today, and just like her sister, I know God has great plans for her. She is artistic and intelligent with an incredible voice. I wait eagerly for His plan to unfold for her. As I pen this, she has graduated from college and works in our hometown. I pray that someday she will use her singing talent, a precious gift from the Lord.

With two children, our available time to drink became minimal, but we managed on occasion while I also started attending church with the girls more frequently. My pastor came to my home once and asked if I knew what it meant to have my children dedicated to the Lord, and I did. I just was not sure how to do it all correctly. I was trying though. I wanted them to know Jesus.

CHAPTER THREE

Why, God, Why My Momma?

Once my second daughter was born, I remember asking God why He took my mother when I was only eight years old. I needed her. I sure could have used her help with two daughters. I had so many questions. Life was busy with two young children, a house, and a job, and I still had all that emptiness inside. My children brought me such joy, but I knew something was still missing. I missed my mother terribly during this time and thought of her often.

Earlier in my life, I had horrible dreams, yet I enjoyed those dreams in a sense. In them, I would dig up my mother's grave, and we would go shopping, cook, etc. But morning would come, and I would return her to her grave. I remember wanting to continue each night from the night before.

Perhaps this sounds morbid, but I just wanted to know what life could have been like with my mother. I missed her more than ever before. I became angry at God for taking her. I had been left with a big hole in my heart, and it did not seem too fair. I would watch other moms do things with their children, and I so wanted that. I longed for the closeness of a mother. *Why, God, why did you take my momma?* I would plead as I argued it out with him.

I remember going to drop the girls off at Sunday school in my sporty gray Camaro. I had purchased a standard shift, and I could hardly drive it. I liked it when I saw it and thought, *How hard could it be to learn to drive standard shift anyways?* I squealed the tires many times by mistake. My previous pastor's wife and I would joke about how I would drop my kids off in my gray Camaro, and I hoped I had never squealed driving out of the church parking lot. I found it was quite difficult to drive standard, especially when the vehicle had such power.

One Sunday, I heard a man talking about how he had planned to commit suicide and Jesus helped him. My hair was not fixed, and I was not dressed up, but it did not seem to matter. I sat and listened as this man spoke about his life and the struggles he had, describing how Jesus brought him through. Apparently, several of his family members had committed suicide, and he had contemplated doing the same. I began thinking that perhaps Jesus could help me too. I thought perhaps he could take away my pain. I started going to church more frequently, and we partied less on weekends when I realized I could not go to church *and* party all weekend. My girls were involved in the Christmas programs, and I found myself at church more frequently. Thank you, Jesus. It is true then that "a child shall lead them."

Another two years passed, and I became pregnant once again. As with my first daughter, I loved being pregnant, and it was very special carrying a child in my womb. On August 22, 1989, I was induced into labor and my beautiful brown-haired, brown-eyed daughter was born. It took a while for us to decide what her name should be. We had contemplated naming her after her father's grandmother, but she looked more like a Brooke than a Bertha. My then-husband's grandfather was disappointed, but he just sighed and said, "Why didn't you name her something simple, like Nellie or something?" He sure brought us a lot of laughs while expressing his disappointment in us naming her differently than his heart's desire.

For the third time, we had our daughter dedicated to the Lord, and she completed our family. She is another very intelligent, creative girl, and she has a neat sense of humor. I so look forward to watching her gifts and talents unfold as she walks into her destiny. As I pen this, she is married and the mother of a little handsome guy named Emmett and a beautiful, brown-eyed baby girl, just like her.

It hardly seems possible that all three of my children are married with children of their own now. My middle daughter also married and has a beautiful daughter named Maisie Grace, a handsome son, and a bonus daughter from her husband's previous relationship. It seems like yesterday that they were little girls. I used to dress them all alike with lacy anklets and petticoats under their dresses. I would curl their hair, and they all looked so beautiful. Then, the teen years came, along with minds of their very own, and the dresses became a thing of the past. Their closets filled with jeans, and they began their journeys to discover what they believed. I rest assured that God's Word will come to pass in their lives. I pray for them each day and trust that my Jesus is watching over them. I look forward to watching Him fulfill the destiny that He has planned for each one of their lives. I know they all will be used in ministry someday. My prayer is that day will be very soon and that God will give them an encounter of Himself, one that proves to them without a shadow of a doubt that He is real and wants to be the Savior of their lives. Today I pray, believe for them, and wait expectantly for the plan of God to be released into their lives. I know prayer changes things.

CHAPTER FOUR

I Met Him

My life was extremely busy when my children were young. I was working full-time and taking care of three children, not to mention dealing with the pain still buried deep inside me. My then-husband had an accident and was out of work.

That was my life for seven years.

My now then-husband became the housekeeper and cook during that time while I went out and worked. I grew quite resentful. I never really wanted to work outside the home and leave my girls. My resentment only added to the pain I continued to bury deep within.

One Sunday morning, I rededicated my life to the Lord, and I began a new adventure. This journey brought healing, deliverance, and restoration to my life. The journey would be full of trials, yet it would bring me such joy and happiness that I would want to share it with the whole world.

I can truly say, thank you, Jesus, for the trials in my life, for without them, I would never have known you as my Father and my Friend.

I have always been the type of individual who goes all in. There's no medium speed for me. After my rededication, I was all in for Jesus. I told everyone I could about Him. I wanted everyone to know Him like I knew Him. Much to my surprise, it did not take long for religious folks to become uncomfortable. Some folks thought I was odd because I made statements like, "God said . . ." or "God led me to . . ." I thought everyone whose life was dedicated to God heard His voice like I did, but I quickly learned that you had to be careful about who you shared certain things like that with, even within the church. Not everyone who goes to church is His, and not everyone hears his voice.

While I was more careful about exactly what I shared, I did not stop sharing. I share Jesus with people just as much today as I did back then, if not more. I simply learned to use more love, forgiveness, and prayer when I share Him.

I find it sad that there is so much religion in the world and not enough relationship. My heart ached at mistreatment from the church, and I can only imagine the grief it causes my Heavenly Father. Thank you, Lord, for being a God of mercy, grace, and long-suffering.

His Word states, "My sheep hear My voice, and I know them, and they follow Me." (John 10:27) If you are not hearing His voice, you may want to ask Him why. Be sure you are in the Kingdom, for you should not be deaf to His voice. Are you truly His child? I frequently ask people these questions. It's a good practice for us to examine ourselves and find the answers.

After my rededication, I began to believe His Word. If the Word said it, I accepted it—no ifs, ands, or buts about it. I'm frankly astonished by the amount of unbelief in the Body of Christ—the church in general—today. I hear a lot of "God doesn't this anymore" or "God doesn't that anymore" or "That was in the Old Testament, which is not for today." Lord, forgive the unbelievers, for they know not what they do. You are the same God yesterday, today, and forever. You have never changed, and, yes, "I can do all things through Christ who strengthens me." (Philippians 4:13) I choose to forgive those who say I cannot do all things. Lord, forgive our unbelief. Forgive me for the times I did not believe

You either. Give us all grace and guide us to trust You more, I pray. Bring your church to this place, Lord, that we can take You at Your Word. You have so much more for us as the Body of Christ, and I pray we will walk in our full inheritance. Teach us Lord, I pray.

As my journey with Jesus continued, He started to make changes in my life. He began to deal with my past and bring healing and deliverance. It was not instantaneous healing. Jesus brought my healing line by line, precept by precept. He showed me the lies I believed and revealed the truth.

I always wondered how some folks get saved one day and enter ministry the next. I loved Jesus with all my heart, and it was still a long journey of healing that continues to this day. I couldn't have entered ministry any earlier than I did. In next chapters, I share events, circumstances, and scriptures the Lord used to bring deliverance, healing, and restoration to my life. His ways are sovereign, and I will forever be grateful for the journey I am on with Him.

If He would have changed everything for me instantaneously, I would not be writing today nor sharing how Jesus can heal every area for which you need wholeness in your life. He is capable of taking good care of His people. He is a good God—all the time. He promises that His love and mercy will follow us all the days of our lives.

Can you believe that blessing?

CHAPTER FIVE

The Brown Paper Bag

The first healing I received from the Lord was for my reaction to getting sick. When I got sick in any way, I would hyperventilate and lose feeling in my hands and feet. It was such a strong reaction that I had to go to the emergency room so that the doctors could give me something to relax. At times, I would need to breathe into a brown paper bag—the stereotypical panic attack. Breathing into a brown paper bag was the most embarrassing part for me, but my panic was real, and the bag was necessary sometimes. I always felt like I was going to die. I would try to fight it, but every single time I got sick, the same thing happened.

On one occasion, my then-husband refused to drive me to the emergency room, as I'm sure he was tired of the same routine. So, I drove myself to the emergency room in my nightgown, bathroom trash can wedged between my legs to use on the way. I had to keep pulling over to the side of the road to vomit, and I could not feel my hands or feet. As I mentioned earlier, my hands would curl up and ache. Once or twice my then-mother-in-law came to the hospital, and she would rub my hands and feet, but no one really knew how much they pained me. And this time, I was on my own. When I arrived at the emergency room, they took me in right away. I did not even have to wait in the lobby. I guess that's the secret to fast emergency room service—go in your nightgown, carry a barf bucket, and you are not suitable for the waiting area. I felt really foolish, but this was my reality, and I had to live in it.

At the time, my oldest daughter was around two, and my middle daughter was just a baby. I know my panic attacks must have been frightening for them. My sister and I walked together often early in the mornings, and one day I asked her if she knew why I had these panic attacks. I did not see this happening to anyone else. I had not met anyone else living with anxiety, and

I was as tired of my trips to the emergency room as my then-husband. My sister didn't have any answer for me, so I told her I was going to talk to Jesus about it.

I prayed about my panic attacks over the next few weeks. Then one day, as I was on my knees beside my bed praying, I had a sudden memory. I remembered being a young girl seeing my mother lying on the floor, gasping for breath. I remembered being frightened and running upstairs. I heard the ambulance come and take her away . . . and my mother never came home.

Somehow, I had buried this memory in my subconscious. Seeing that happen to my mother had frightened me to the point that when I got sick, I thought I was going to die too. A spirit of death had attached itself to me.

Once I realized what was going on, the healing began. I knew I had nothing to fear as far as death. I loved Jesus, and if anything ever happened to me, I was going home to be with Him. This is what I live for. I loved Jesus with all my heart, and I was doing my very best to walk with Him the best I knew how. With this sudden memory, I believe the Lord showed me the root of the problem I had been dealing with almost my whole life. The next time I was sick, I intentionally thanked the Lord that someday I would go to be with Him and spend eternity with the One I love and I live my life for. I spoke His Word, and although I still got sick, I never hyperventilated again. Thank you, Jesus, for revealing truth. You truly are a healing Jesus.

If you fear death, know that is not the will of your Father. He loves you and is watching over you until you go to be with Him. There is nothing for a born-again believer to fear. Fear is not from God, and you can be set free. Jesus can—and will—deliver you. Fear has no place in your life.

One of my favorite healing Scriptures is Psalm 107:20: "He sent His word and healed them, And delivered them from their destructions." This was the first healing that I received from the Lord. In the years that followed, I received other healings that I share in later chapters. Believe in Him and His Word if you need healing, too.

"O Death, where is your sting?" (1 Corinthians 15:55)

CHAPTER SIX

Not the Blue Lights

The next fear the Lord would free me from was my fear of the police. Perhaps this sounds extreme, but I was truly petrified of the police. When I saw a police officer, my heart would pound. I was terrified.

When my then-husband was injured and had to stay home with the girls, I was working full-time at the local housing authority, and I occasionally had to deal with the police. I was better at hiding my fear than I had when I feared getting sick. To deal with the police, I would go to the bathroom and practice my breathing right before I met with them.

Once again, I turned to my sister for answers, and once again, she didn't have them. She didn't know why I was afraid of police. I was learning from the Word of God that fear was not from Him. Fear is not my portion, and it is not your portion either. I realized that I did not need to be afraid of the police, so again, I began to pray about the issue. And again, one day I was kneeling beside my bed when I had a flashback of an incident from my childhood.

When I was young, my sister was very protective of me—overly and obsessively protective. She tried hard to keep alcohol out of our home, and I am thankful for that. I remembered being a young girl, and one day my dad and another relative were in the basement drinking. My sister told them they had to leave, and when they refused, she called the police. The police came and escorted them out of our home. I don't remember if they took them to the police station or just away from the house, but it was terrifying for a young girl to see her father taken away by the police. I had buried the memory somewhere deep within like so many others, but my subconscious remembered the trauma; therefore, whenever I saw the police, fear rose in me.

Again, I took God's Word to heart, which says I have no reason to fear. I chose to believe the promises of God and use them to replace my fear until I was no longer frightened of the police. Remembering this incident helped me see how fear had gained entrance into my life. "There is no fear in love; but perfect love casts out fear . . . " (1 John 4:18) I knew Jesus' love for me was perfect and I did not have to be afraid. Again, His Word brought deliverance.

Sometimes when we believe lies, God sheds light on what is going on through the power of His Holy Spirit so that we can live free. We can dispel the lie with God's truth.

I know my sister was doing the best she knew how at the time, and in many ways, she did the right thing. She suffered growing up with an alcoholic father and other relatives with the same addiction, and I appreciated her trying to protect me from the effects of alcoholism as a child. I know she saved me from a great deal (more about her in a later chapter).

With the blessing of that memory, another fear had been conquered. Jesus was setting me free one deliverance at a time.

I am so thankful that His love for me is unconditional. I loved Him with all I had and lived for Him the best I knew how, but I was still in bondage. Layer by layer, He began gently revealing truth to me. Jesus loves His children, and I am His child. He began to restore the things that had been taken away from me.

For the first time in my life, I had peace about dying. No more hyperventilating, no more losing feeling in my hands and feet, and no more trips to the emergency room for medication. Peace, sweet peace!

I also no longer feared the police. Do you realize how many police are on the road, in the stores, etc.? I can laugh about it now, but when I still feared the police, anxiety would swell up inside of me until it caused a panic. Now all of that is replaced with peace. Today, I see police officers and smile—as long as they do not have their blue lights turned on behind me. I am thankful for the protection and service they provide to our communities. I even now pray for them on occasion.

Fear for peace is an incredible trade. This is what Jesus died on the Cross for. What a price He paid.

Why would I fear anything if I truly understand what He has done for me and what my inheritance is as a born-again believer?

How can we ever say *thank you* to Him?

Personally, I have learned some ways to thank Him. I spend time with Him, both in His Word and in His presence. Sometimes I just sing songs and worship Him. I tell Him how much He means to me and that I am so thankful He died for me while I was yet a sinner. I continually try to be a thankful person, for with Him I have it all. Material items and wealth on earth just seem so insignificant compared to His anointing and His glory. Yes, Lord, that's what we desire.

Do you feel like dancing from the joy of it all?

Dancing...

My Lord, My God, My Redeemer
My Father and yet my Friend.
I wait upon You . . .
I look to You, Oh Lord
Wisdom, yes, I lack.
I ask of You, my Lord . . .
Healing Waters—yes, I do believe
Healing your people—wholeness
That's what we so desire.
You, Oh Lord, You are the one . . .
The only one, who can complete the deep work in me.
Removing pain, shame, deception
Bringing truth to the light . . .
Yes, Lord, that's what we need
Strongholds destroyed by the power of Your name.
Jesus, how do we say *thank you*?
I want to worship You day and night
Never forgetting the brokenness and how You turned my darkness into light.
Dancing, dancing, I want to praise Your name.
Inside I'm dancing both day and night.

Jesus, my Lord, I just want You to know, how much
I love You.
Jesus my friend and yet my Lord . . .
I wait on You.
I feel like dancing as I wait on You . . .
I feel like dancing as I wait on You . . .

~~~~~~~~~~~~~~~~~~~~~~~~~~~~~~~~~~~~~

Another way I show my Jesus love is to cherish His people. I pray each day, "Lord, send the people you need to in my path today." He has brought a diverse group of people for me to cherish—poor people, homeless people, broken people, discouraged people, sick people, hurting people. While there have been times the smell makes me feel ill, I know these are the folks Jesus would minister to if He were here today. I love Him so much and want to be a vessel He can use for His glory. What I want to do with my life is what Jesus did when He lived here on earth.

In the next chapter, I talk about some of the folks Jesus has brought into my life. My prayer is that each and every one of them—and you—will desire a deeper relationship with Jesus. He makes my life exciting, a journey that I hope your heart will also desire.

CHAPTER SEVEN

Alice, Please Bake the Pie

I once knew a woman who struggled with alcoholism. I will call her Alice for the sake of privacy. She had long, stringy, unkempt hair, was very thin, and had a big wart on her nose. She resembled a stereotypical picture of a witch; however, Alice was no witch. She was a woman who lived in an apartment by herself and did not keep it very clean. Her refrigerator was always empty of anything other than the beer that filled the shelves. People always complained about Alice. She would walk to the store, and you could not offer her a ride if you saw her because she was known to urinate in people's vehicles. People continually whined about Alice, but I tried to help her. On one occasion, I had the opportunity to sit down and talk with Alice. She had been through so much in her life; it was no wonder that she drank to suppress the pain. Alice could not read or write, and she had no formal education. She was basically a loner. Her friends were few, but her doubters were many, so I began to pray for Alice.

One Christmas, I put Alice's name on the church list for a food basket. A neighbor told me that she took Alice a pumpkin pie, and Alice asked her why it was so runny. The pie was a frozen, uncooked pie, and it turns out that Alice had not cooked the pie and was trying to eat it the way it came in the box. It was of course quite runny, and she was having difficulty eating it. Can you imagine how awful that must have tasted?

On one Christmas Eve, my daughter and I took her some gifts. Knowing she did not have anything, we brought her some towels and some pillows for her bed. I know she appreciated the gifts. I continued to pray for Alice. My heart ached for her. I thought my life was hard, yet here was Alice, who left home at twelve years of age. After she shared just a small part of her life story with me, I knew Alice was using alcohol to bury the pain in her life. I continued to pray and to reach out to her in an attempt to make life a little easier for her.

One day, I received a phone call that she was quite ill and needed to go to the hospital, but she refused to go by ambulance. I was unable to take her since I was at work, so I put my head down on my desk and prayed, asking my Heavenly Father to make a way for this dear lady. After approximately twenty minutes, I received a phone call from a relative of Alice's who said she would take her to the hospital.

Thank you, Jesus. You do answer prayer.

I also asked some men from our church to go pray for Alice and talk to her about Jesus. I was not confident enough to lead her in prayer back then. I now realize that no matter your level of experience, the Holy Spirit will help you. God looks at the heart. We're often taught formulas for prayer and the born-again life that we struggle to remember when it's not a formula at all. For example, one man took Alice a small stuffed animal. I am almost certain that was the only stuffed animal that Alice had ever received, and there's no formula that could have dictated that.

I went to visit Alice one day, and her room was empty. I knew that she had died. I came home, laid on my bed, and cried. I knew she was with Jesus and that her life was full of joy. She was free from the pain that this world had brought her. I had prayed so much for her over the course of a year that I felt as if I were losing a sister. In essence, I was. I know that as I write this today, Alice is in Heaven. The Lord has given me that assurance. I know that the Lord did not put her in my path by mistake. He used her to teach me a great deal. There was no funeral, no calling hours, and no flowers. Her belongings all went into the dumpster. The Lord showed me how the alcohol was keeping the pain down in her life, but He also told me to look past the alcohol and into her heart. She had no status in this world. She had no assets, friends, or relatives who acknowledged her. She did have a son who I had met once. When we met, he told me that one time when he was younger, Alice was going to jump off a moving truck to commit suicide, but he stopped her. He smelled of alcohol too.

I remember praying, "Lord, thank you for saving her. You breathed life into her, and we are commanded to love Your people. Help Your church to love each other. Lord, teach me to love others, too."

On another occasion, I was watching Joyce Meyer teach about the favor of God on television. She said to pray before you go out to eat, etc. and ask for the favor of the Lord. I thought that sounded like a great idea. I shared this teaching with my family, we prayed, and then off to the restaurant we went. Our waitress was not a very good one the night I shared that teaching. She said things like, "You don't want desert tonight, do you?"

She would take her hand and wipe her mouth, sweat beading off her face. My family said, "Oh Mom, see you really have the favor of God. Oh yeah, this prayer really worked." We laughed and went home. Somehow, God gave us the grace to say nothing and still leave her a tip. I respect Joyce Meyer, and I know that she is a woman of the Word, so I kept at it.

The next time we went out to eat, I prayed, "Father, I ask you for favor, the favor of God. Lord, I pray that we have a good meal and a good time together, in Jesus' name, amen." That seemed like a simple enough prayer, right? Off we went, and we decided to try the same restaurant, again.

We were seated, and our waitress appeared, and yes, you guessed it, it was the same waitress as the last time. I was really struggling with this scenario because I know God answers prayer. I kept thinking, "What's up with this, Jesus?"

We ordered our food, and the girls and my then-husband were really ribbing me, "Ha, ha, Mom, your prayer really works." When the waitress brought our food, she smelled terrible and had her thumb in one of our mashed potatoes. All we could do was laugh. We ate the best we could and went home, but I had to pull over to vomit on the way home because all I could think of was the thumb in the potatoes. By the time we reached home, my stomach was as empty as it was before I had left.

But I had prayed.

I struggled to understand the ways of God. I wanted to understand why He was doing this. The Scriptures tells us that His ways are higher than our ways, and His thoughts are higher than our thoughts.

A few weeks passed, and I received a call from a friend. She wanted to know if I could get together and pray with a hurting woman. She said she had picked up a woman who was suicidal and wanted to bring her to prayer. I felt like I was supposed to go, so I took my Bible, and off I went.

When I arrived, I was surprised. The lady I was going to pray with was the waitress who had her thumb in the potatoes. I was so thankful that the Lord had given our family the grace not to complain about her and to tip her appropriately. How could I ever talk to her about Jesus if we had caused her more pain in her life? I learned a valuable lesson that night. Whomever Jesus sends to your life, treat them as if Jesus were standing there with you. Jesus lives in you. Where you go, he is also there. I would have missed a divine appointment that Jesus was setting up if I had allowed my flesh to be in control.

We think we deserve what we pay for, and we expect good service from others, but these are habits the Lord wants to break us of. No, my family did not get good service, and no, we did not get what we paid for, but did Jesus get what He paid for when He walked here on earth? Thank you, Jesus, for teaching me that it is okay for us not to get what we deserve or pay for.

We went out to eat on another occasion to the same restaurant, and no, you did not guess it, we had a different waitress. The first waitress was there, and she came over and spoke to us. Her previous behavior did not seem to matter much anymore. She had given her life to the Lord, and I was happy. She had been through a lot too. Alcohol, men, and poverty caused some of the pain in her life.

The waitress has since left that restaurant, and though I do not know where she is today, I know the Lord will continue to bring healing and deliverance to her life. She is another sister in Christ, another interesting stopping place on my journey with Jesus.

Thank you for my life's journey and for teaching me Your heart, oh Lord. May we continue to be vessels You can use to bring Your will here on earth. You walk close to the brokenhearted, the poor and hurting. May we walk close to them, too, oh Lord. May we have Your compassion for the world around us, I pray.

After my experiences with Alice and the waitress, I wrote the following narrative.

Compassion

My sister, your countenance looks downcast, your face does reflect.

Your burden looks heavy, your load—is it too much
to carry alone?

For you, my friend, God has sent His Son, and He
also sent me your way.
I'm His love extended to you. How can I help you
today?

If you want to share your burden, I know Jesus will
give you the strength to overcome.
You will have the victory.

As we journey the path of life together,
We have many a trial.
Jesus gave you to me, my sister,
To love you and to be his love vial.

I want to help you bandage your wounds
Until Jesus heals you where you hurt.

You see, my sister, my friend, we all walk through
pain
And the storms, they do blow.

But, together with Jesus,
In Him, we both will grow.

This poem reflects my love for Alice and the waitress. It communicates that the Lord not only answers our prayers but is also the Great Physician and healer of the wounded heart. Through these experiences, the Lord taught me that I could use my pain to help others. Through prayer, God took Alice's poverty and turned it into the incredible wealth of knowing Him. Today she is with Him in Paradise and is no longer enslaved by an addiction to alcohol. She is free, and free indeed, in Christ. As of this writing, I haven't seen the waitress, but I trust she is continuing her walk with the Lord.

CHAPTER EIGHT

Righteous? Are You Talking to Me?

Many years ago, I went to see Joyce Meyers speak in Springfield, Massachusetts. This was like a dream come true for me. I was so excited for the opportunity to go. As my friend and I were getting ready to depart, I will never forget how thankful I was that I was going to hear a woman speak who I admired as much as Joyce. She is so real.

When I listened to her program each day, I learned that I was the righteousness of God because of the blood of Jesus Christ. She was the main person who taught me about my identity in Jesus Christ through her programs. Do you know how many Christians and preachers think that you have to be perfect to be righteous? When I heard Joyce's testimony and how much Jesus had done for her, I was encouraged to pursue Him again with everything I had. I was especially thankful for her honesty about her struggles, including the ones she had overcome. She is such an anointed teacher. I have never met her personally, although her husband, Dave, signed a coffee mug as a gift for my sister. Someday I hope to personally meet them.

When I was packing the van to leave for our trip, Alyssa, my middle child who was in first grade at the time, begged to go with me, but my then-husband didn't think we could afford for her to go. As I was trying to get out the door, she wrapped her arms around my legs and wouldn't let go. I asked my then-husband to reconsider since it wouldn't cost very much for a few hamburger happy meals. We were staying with my brother, so that was free, and Joyce's teaching was free too, so the cost was minimal. He finally agreed to let her go with me.

I will never forget her expression as we packed her up quickly to depart. She cried from Presque Isle almost to Houlton, which is about an hour's drive. I asked her why she was crying, and she said she was so happy that she could go. It was there at Joyce Meyer's conference that Alyssa felt the call of God on her life. She also experienced God for herself in ways that no person could have ever taught her. That was in 1994, the same year Alyssa was Little Miss Presque Isle.

In between Joyce's sessions, we went to eat at a nearby mall food court. We saw a homeless woman, and I told Alyssa that we needed to buy her lunch. She said, "Oh Mama, we can't. We don't have enough money. Remember, Mom, we only have a little money?"

I said, "Alyssa, if Jesus was here today and saw this hungry person, what would He do?"

She responded immediately, "Mama, buy her lunch."

The lady got in line before us, and we paid for her meal. The woman behind the counter commented on how nice that was. She told us that the homeless woman never bothered anyone; she just had a hard time and lost her place to live. The woman behind the counter said she was the nicest homeless person you would ever meet. I know Alyssa will never forget this experience, and I believe this was my first real heart-to-heart connection with the homeless.

On that same trip, I remember Joyce teaching about dying to the self. I thought, *Oh Joyce, I came all the way here to hear you say that I need to die more?* But I gave the Holy Spirit permission to do the work He needed to do, and He showed me where I had not surrendered completely. My flesh was alive in many ways in 1994. Here we are, many years later, and I'm still asking, "Am I dead yet?"

Lord, I surrender my life to You, and I encourage everyone else to surrender as well. He has a great plan for your life, and as you read this, you can see how He is fulfilling the desires of my heart and the plan He has for me. I believe God plants desire in our heart and works with us until it is accomplished. We all have a destiny, a plan, and a purpose.

There was one other time I was blessed enough to attend a Joyce Meyer conference, and I drove another friend who wanted to attend. I could write a whole book about that adventure. We both put all our money in the offering plate to help Joyce spread the good news and had no money for gas, tolls, etc. on our way home. We had to write a check just to get out of the parking garage. Oops! It's a long way from Springfield home to Presque Isle, but we managed to make it. Some toll booth personnel put money in for us when we asked them if they could accept a check.

Oh, and then there were the blue lights and the shampoo bottle. When I got pulled over, I said, "No, Officer, I was not drinking," as I passed him my shampoo bottle. I had been looking for loose change for the next toll in my cosmetic bag.

He replied, "Oh, I thought for sure I had you."

That definitely did not feel like a destiny moment.

CHAPTER NINE

Meet My Parents

My mother got married when she was only fourteen years old. I can barely fathom that. I'm told she was a kind woman. I asked the Lord about her kindness one day, and He reminded me that kindness is a fruit of the Spirit. May we all be remembered as kind. I'm also told she gave her heart to the Lord at a church service in Allagash, Maine. My mother was born and raised in that town of approximately two hundred people. She had fourteen pregnancies. One ended with a stillborn child, and one child passed away at eighteen months. She had one developmentally delayed child and one physically handicapped child. Twelve children are a lot to care for, and I am sure she had her hands full with the extra needs of my two beautiful special sisters.

My mother did not have an easy life. I have a few memories of her, but I know I will see her in Heaven one day. The Lord gave me confirmation of it one day during a church service. There were some ladies who attended the church who were involved in a car accident, and two of the ladies died. I didn't know them well, but I grieved for their families. We had a special singer at that church, and it became plain to me as she sang that day that my mother was in Heaven and that I would see her again. At the time, I did not know that my mother had been a born-again believer in Jesus Christ, but I've had peace about my mother's death since that day.

After church service on a Sunday late one June, I decided to take a drive to my mother's graveside and put some flowers on her and my father's burial plot. I drove the two hours alone, praising the Lord and worshipping Him for His goodness. I will never forget that day. No one from my household wanted to come along, but a relative from another part of Maine was at the cemetery as well. We talked about my mother, and this relative invited me to come back with her to her mother's home. It was then that I learned my mother was spirit-filled.

No one knew I had asked the Lord for the opportunity to know. He is faithful and will answer when we ask. Thank you, Jesus. Although I look most like my father, I was pleased to discover that I share a great likeness to my mother in our faith and anointed lives.

My father was an uneducated man. Something happened at school one day when he was young, and he never went back. His education consisted of just that, one day. Consequently, he could not read or write very well. I remember my father most for his coffee brandy, which I'm sure was to keep the pain buried deep as I know his life was filled with pain and disappointment. He worked in the woods cutting trees for many years. I remember my brother saying that Dad made a fire to warm his tea when my brother worked in the woods with him. Growing up, I always felt Dad was an old man. He was almost fifty when I was born. Now, fifty seems quite young to me. I was with my dad when he passed away. He did say he was ready to go, and only he would know that for sure. After his death, we found a Bible from my former pastor. Inside, he had written the steps my father needed to take to go to Heaven.

It's hard to put into words how I felt the day he passed away. I try to accept things for the way they are without adding too many emotions. I remember standing beside my father's bed when the alarm went off on the monitor and he took his last breath. I can still see that in my mind so clearly today. I was naming all the children and grandchildren I knew and told him that they all loved him.

I had never felt close to my father. He thought the same way most people do—what others give you shows their love for you. What a lie. What others really want is you.

My father gave me alcohol as a teenager. When I would get caught, he would say that I stole it from him. He had a girlfriend who would buy alcohol for me too. I see where I am today, and I look around at a second and third generation of alcoholics in my family. I am so blessed to be free from that bondage. As I kept walking with the Lord and surrendering all I knew to Him, He took off layer after layer of bondage. I am thankful that the generational curse of alcohol has been broken in my life. To God be all the glory, for His word is true.

> *Therefore, if the Son makes you free, you shall be free indeed.* —John 8:36

CHAPTER TEN

Giving and My Sister

Jen was the oldest girl in my family, born when my mother was only fourteen years old. She weighed in at two pounds and was born with a rare bone disease. Her world was different than most due to her illness and the many trials she would endure. She was like a very, very, very strict mother to me, but she was also a unique individual, and I feel blessed that her life touched mine. I thank God today that she was my sister, although it was both a privilege and exhausting.

My sister loved Jesus, but Jen did not know how much Jesus loved her. I wish we had more time together. She lived almost three hours away, but we spoke on the phone several times a day. She passed away a few years ago, and all that is left are memories. I would get so annoyed when she called frequently. I would be on my way to work or taking my children to an activity or school and she would call. Now, I will never hear her voice again.

I never knew how much pain she was in physically and spiritually until after her death. Sometimes our family members are the hardest to reach with our ministry. I was told after her death, by her hairdresser, that Jen never felt loved by Jesus. She knew He loved others, but she could not feel His love for her. That saddened this sister's heart to hear.

Jen liked to watch Joyce Meyer too, and we often shared Joyce stories. I had the opportunity to attend a Joyce Meyer conference twice and offered to take Jen with me, but she declined. Jen wrote children's books and worked hard at selling and donating them.

She was so much more than a sister to me. She told me many times that I was like her own child, as she could not have any, and she helped raise me. She tried hard to protect me and give me the things I needed. I know many times she and my other siblings went without just to give me extra. I wish life would have been easier for her and my family.

Jen loved to sing country and western music, and she wrote songs as well. She had a heart for homeless people, those living on the streets. She always told me stories about talking to them, and she would give them blankets and food. She shared just about everything she had, from her own makeup to turkeys. When I would visit, sometimes she would send me to McDonald's to get milkshakes for the neighbors in wheelchairs who could not get there themselves. I would go to the grocery store for her and others who had special needs. Then she would want to go to the local thrift stores too.

I did not realize the depth of her heart back then.

I do today.

I guess I was always just a bit frustrated at the added responsibility for me, but her heart was right, and I am thankful that she looked out for others. She did not hold onto anything too tightly. I see quite a few similarities in our lives today.

Father, may I always prefer others over myself. Forgive me for the times I have not. May You, Lord, complete the work in me so that I will be a giver. I desire a blessed life, a channel through which You can filter the needs of others. Let it be so, Jesus.

CHAPTER ELEVEN

My Secret Shame

In the 1990s, a couple come to our church to minister about miscarriages. I remember that evening like it was yesterday. They were a young couple who were unable to have children. They sang and then spoke about different issues in marriage. They dedicated particular songs to people who had lost a child or had an abortion.

During the song dedications, I began to weep. I cried all through the evening meeting.

I went home from that meeting feeling broken up inside. It is very hard to put into words what I was feeling. I wanted to die to get rid of the pain. I cried all night long. I screamed. I got down on my knees beside my bed and prayed. I realized for the very first time that the choice I made wasn't a good one. Although I had never really understood before, I chose to take the life of a baby when there were others who would do anything to have a baby. I bought into the lie that the baby in my womb was just tissue. I had buried the pain from the abortion.

My then-husband and I never spoke about the abortion. No one knew this secret hidden deep within my heart. I didn't really think much about it until the couple came to our church. Life was moving forward, and I thought everything with my abortion was finished. I made the choice, and nothing could bring my child back to me. I missed him so much that night. I remember just sobbing for hours. My then-husband tried to talk to me about it, but what he had to say did not matter to me. He could not take the pain away. No matter how hard he tried to comfort me, it did not seem to help.

The next morning, the Lord led me to call a friend from my church and share my abortion experience with her. I argued with the Holy Spirit for a few hours, but I ultimately knew the importance of being obedient. I called her and explained that I had something to share that was so ugly that if she decided not to be my friend, I would understand. I took a deep breath and told her about the abortion I had when I was a teenager and how I never told anyone. I told her about the church meeting I attended and how broken I was. She began to weep. My friend had also had an abortion and never told anyone.

I can't begin to express how I felt about what happened that day. I confessed the abortion to her, and all that pain and brokenness inside me simply vanished. The secret I had buried and carried was out. The Bible says that everything done in darkness will be brought to light. I am so thankful that the Lord forgives our sins. I learned that we can never out-sin Jesus. I do not want to sin, and I try not to, but when I do, I am so thankful that God gave His only Son, Jesus, to pay that price. I do not want to hurt Him because I have a great love for Him. When you have felt the pain of brokenness, know there is no person who can make you whole again, and experience the touch of Jesus on your life, you no longer want to sin.

Abortion isn't the answer, but I had already done it. I know today how great that sin is. When I look at my three beautiful daughters, I know the Lord has blessed me beyond what I could have imagined. Someone once told me that the Lord gave me three girls because He wanted me to know what it was like to be a mother and have a mother-daughter relationship. Some people say

God punishes those who commit such a sin as abortion, but that is not the case. He died for us while we were yet sinners. That is so hard for people to grasp, especially the more religious folks.

I remember writing "My Father's Love"—my first writing. That was the day I truly started to grasp His love for me. He died for me when I was deep in the mire of premarital sex, abortion, and drunkenness. That was years earlier in my life, but it was all paid for by the precious blood of Jesus Christ.

I wish I had made wiser choices. I wish I had never experienced the pain and trauma of abortion and its aftermath. I wish I had never messed with alcohol, and I wish a whole lot of other things would have been different—but they are not.

I have learned to turn those poor choices over to Jesus and allow Him to use those experiences to help others. Jesus took all the pain out of my heart the day I confessed my abortion to my friend. Something supernatural happened that day. I had a hidden secret that I did not even realize was keeping me in bondage.

After my initial confession, I told my pastor about the abortion, and as God brought other women into my life who had the same stamp on their past, I shared my story with them. Then I felt the Lord wanted me to share this healing in a book. He wants to use my testimony to help others heal too.

Several years ago, I volunteered at my local Pregnancy Care Center. I felt led to sign up for their training. I did not need another event on my calendar, but I really felt that Jesus wanted me to go. It was at their training center that I met another post-abortive woman.

One day, the center's director called to tell me about training being offered to help post-abortive women. A dear lady paid all our expenses to go to this training, and she went with us. This training was three hours south. I was sure God had set this up. It was this training experience that led me to a study *Forgiven and Set Free* by Linda Cochrane, a book that would take me deeper into healing my own abortion.

Prior to this training, I had never named my child; I had no memory of him. I didn't think about him too much. But it was time for me to go deeper in the abortion aftermath. I did my study with the other post-abortive woman who was at the center training with me. This pastor's wife became a dear friend as she was going through her own time of healing as well.

I know now that abortion is not the answer.

It leaves a scar that words cannot describe; however, if one has already taken place, I know from personal experience that Jesus can take away the pain and sting. There are consequences to our poor choices—our sins. I won't see my son until I get to Heaven. I can never hear his voice nor see his face in this life.

After my training, I named my son Jeremiah Isaac Murchison. Jeremiah is my favorite book in the Bible. It was through this book that the Lord showed me how He knit me together and created me in my mother's womb, knowing the plan He had for my life. It was right here, in the book of Jeremiah, that he showed me I was wanted, that He wanted me and I was more than the result of a sexual union between two people.

> *"Before I formed you in the womb I knew you; Before you were born I sanctified you; I ordained you a prophet to the nations." Then said I: "Ah, Lord God! Behold, I cannot speak, for I am a youth." But the Lord said to me: "Do not say, 'I am a youth,' For you shall go to all to whom I send you, And whatever I command you, you shall speak. Do not be afraid of their faces, For I am with you to deliver you," says the Lord. Then the Lord put forth His hand and touched my mouth, and the Lord said to me: "Behold, I have put My words in your mouth. See, I have this day set you over the nations and over the kingdoms, To root out and to pull down, To destroy and to throw down, To build and to plant." Moreover the word of the Lord came to me, saying, "Jeremiah,*

what do you see?" And I said, "I see a branch of an almond tree." Then the Lord said to me, "You have seen well, for I am ready to perform My word." And the word of the Lord came to me the second time, saying, "What do you see?" And I said, "I see a boiling pot, and it is facing away from the north." Then the Lord said to me: "Out of the north calamity shall break forth On all the inhabitants of the land. For behold, I am calling All the families of the kingdoms of the north," says the Lord; "They shall come and each one set his throne At the entrance of the gates of Jerusalem, Against all its walls all around, And against all the cities of Judah. I will utter My judgments Against them concerning all their wickedness, Because they have forsaken Me, Burned incense to other gods, And worshiped the works of their own hands. "Therefore prepare yourself and arise, And speak to them all that I command you. Do not be dismayed before their faces, Lest I dismay you before them. For behold, I have made you this day A fortified city and an iron pillar, And bronze walls against the whole land—Against the kings of Judah, Against its princes, Against its priests, And

> *against the people of the land. They will*
> *fight against you, But they shall not prevail*
> *against you. For I am with you," says the*
> *Lord, "to deliver you."* —Jeremiah 1:5–19.

Shortly after the Lord took me through this chapter in Jeremiah, I attended a Women's Aglow Retreat. I was asked to hold up a sign, and a friend took my picture. The sign read: "Before I formed you in the womb I knew you; Before you were born I sanctified you; I ordained you a prophet to the nations." (Jeremiah 1:5)

To that call, I said *yes.* I've never looked back.

I also have a remembrance for my son now. I went to the Christian bookstore when we still had one, and I asked the Lord to help me find a remembrance for Jeremiah. I was drawn to a little Precious Moment boy standing behind a podium. I purchased it, and it sits in my china closet. Precious it is; precious he is. I know he is with his Heavenly Father, and I will see him in Heaven someday. Until then, I pray that the Lord will use me to bring healing to others who have lost a child through abortion, miscarriage, or death. I pray He will use me to help others make a better choice. Abortion is not the answer. It leaves a scar. Oh, does it leave a scar, my friend.

Here I have included some of my writings about my son, Jeremiah. It is hard to express what I have experienced on this journey. As I would write, sometimes the Lord would lead me to a song. Sometimes he would lead me to a person, a scripture. God's leading is the best. He is the best Father any girl could ever ask for. Oh, the love of my Father.

So, let me introduce you to my son, Jeremiah.

Jeremiah,

God knit you together in my womb, knowing the plan ahead for you. He knew I would abort you, and you would be a baby in Heaven.

I am so very sorry for the choice I made. I truly didn't understand. Now that I do, I ask for forgiveness from you, my aborted child.

Jesus has forgiven me, I received His forgiveness, and now I ask the same of you. My decision took away all your rights here on earth and the days you would have enjoyed.

I truly am sorry; I truly feel regret.

I live my life for Christ now; I truly feel His love. The love I thought I would feel from premarital sex didn't fill the void in me.

I was a wounded girl, just looking for love, and I finally found it in Him.

Again, I say, I'm sorry, Jeremiah, my aborted child. Again, I wish I had made a different choice.

I know I will see you in Heaven someday, but until then I will be your voice. May God use me in any way He can to speak regarding life and His plan.

I love you,
Mom

> *"For I know the thoughts that I think toward you," says the Lord, "thoughts of peace and not of evil, to give you a future and a hope."*
> –Jeremiah 29:11

JEREMIAH ISAAC MURCHISON

I believe Jesus gave me this name for you. You were a very special child. You went to Heaven very early in your life. I'm sorry. In the Bible, Isaac was going to be sacrificed, but Jesus provided the sacrifice and spared Isaac. At the time of the abortion, I did not really know I was ending a life. I made the wrong choice. I pray God will use my experience to help others in any way He can. Maybe it will help another woman make a choice not to take her child's life. I'm so sorry it cost you your life here on earth, Jeremiah. You're with Jesus now, and He's the best parent a child could ever have. I have failed many times as a parent. I'm still praying for the perfect remembrance of you to place inside our home, Jeremiah Isaac Murchison, my aborted child.

Mommy loves you; Mommy misses you. I wish I could remember when you went to Heaven. I know it was not winter; it seems like it may have been summer.

A baby that was not born, emptiness inside only Jesus could heal.

Jeremiah, your life will have counted for something as Jesus will open doors for me to speak about the pain and trauma of abortion. Your life was not in vain, my son. Together, women can be set free by Jesus and me.

I so desire for Jesus to use me to bring the love of Christ to the front lines.

Love is not a feeling; love is not sex.

Love is knowing you, oh Lord.

Oh, what a blessing, just knowing you, Lord!

My Son

My son—you cannot see him: abortion took his life.

My son—home with Jesus, I know he's in his Creator's care.

My son—his eyes, his frame, his characteristics I shall never know. I shall never know.

My son, Jeremiah, robbed of his destiny.

Loved, lost, loved again.

Home with Jesus—Heaven.

A baby without a name is now someone—my Jeremiah.

I'm a child growing inside; I know it's hard to understand.

I'm part of you, Mom and Dad.

I'm connected to your womb, Mom. You can't feel me quite yet, but I'm floating all around.

I'm tiny, just beginning to grow.

I'm going to resemble you, Dad and Mom.

I want to be a lot like you.

I can't wait for the nine months to pass so that I can
be a part of your family.
Oh no! Oh no! What's that you say?
NO! NO! Please don't take my life.
I want to be just like you!
Really, I'm not just tissue!
My eyes are formed, and my frame is in place.
Please, Mom, keep me, keep me.
I hear him speak to me.

Jeremiah

~~~~~~

A little while longer, but I must wait to hold you in
my arms
My baby, my aborted son.

I had a connection with you. My womb lay empty. My
heart as well.
You died that day, so did many feelings.

My son, you had no choice; I took it away on that
dark day.
Just tissue so many people would say.
Then why, many years later, does it still feel this way?

Tissue doesn't feel, but I do.
I lost my son, my only son—you.

Creation, I know it's hard to understand
Love between a woman and a man.

Then birth, the blessing from above.
A baby is born, a life, uniqueness designed especially for this day.

I look at His creations
Some tall, some short, some smiling, some sad.

What's wrong, my friend?
Are you missing the child you never had?

Has abortion robbed you of a relationship with your
child? Are you now angry and mad?
YES, YES! I do understand!

You see, I was a young woman who was caught in the
web of deception.
Dark, dark day.

Jeremiah died, my son. Abortion took his life.
Wrong, wrong choice.

Please, listen my friend! Doctors, please take note!
Abortion is not the answer!
Please hear this voice!

My son—I cannot see his eyes. I do not know
His frame, was it most like mine?

Jeremiah died a life without a choice.
A baby with no voice.
More than Jeremiah died that day.
A part of me, now my womb lay empty and oh so bare.

My heart froze, feelings buried, pain and trauma left behind.
Abortion—not the right choice.

SCARS

You can't see my scars—they are hidden deep within.
You say I look so nice, and you think I'm doing oh
so well.

My scar is oozing with pain, hurt, and despair.
Does anyone even realize the pain I can hardly bear?

My scar you cannot see. My countenance does reflect
A bad choice, a dark day.
My scar, I'm left with feelings of shame and guilt.
If abortion is the right choice, then why all the pain?

My choice, my decision, my rights.
I've made my choice; now I hurt.

Many years later, I ask, when does the pain end?
I thought it was just tissue, no real life.

No! No! Please don't buy that lie!
It leaves a scar.

You can't change it for me. Medication can probably
ease the pain for a time, but then what's the course?

Abortion, scars, pain, and regret

Please consider offering alternatives

Scars—marred for life

Don't recommend abortion—it's all about life!

CHAPTER TWELVE

Left Hook, Right Hook

I almost forgot to introduce one of my other sisters, Ethel, and that would not be good. If she were here, I would get a right or left hook for omitting her. She didn't speak, but she sure was powerful with her fists. She was born without a thyroid—a special needs child who had great purpose and destiny. She taught us more about life than what we could ever read in a book.

Everything was Ethel's way and her way only. She could not see anything different than that. We learned to adapt quite quickly because of her right and left hook approach. It was no wonder her nickname became Hooky.

Being from a poor family, our Christmas gifts were usually donated. I am so thankful for agencies that donate to families who don't have much, and I really want to stop and say *thank you* on behalf of all the folks who ever received gifts from others. Maybe you who donated never received a *thank you*, but the God who sees everything knows all you have done. His Word tells us that He is the rewarder of all that is done in secret.

One year, my uncle bought me a round radio for Christmas. It was white, and it was from Radio Shack. I sure did love that radio. It is the only gift I remember receiving that was not donated. I may have received others, but it takes several good memories to cancel one negative memory, so this is the good one I remember.

Can you guess who wanted the little round, white radio? I bet you can.

I gave Ethel the radio maybe not with the best attitude since I was only a child, but we always tried to make life easier for her. Also, remember, Hooky got what she wanted if we could all make it happen.

It has been many years since Ethel was reunited with our mom in Heaven. One night in recent years, I was having a little chat with Jesus about my sister, Hooky. Life was difficult for her without a voice. As I discussed her life issues with Him, I asked the Lord, "Remember the radio she wanted? She must have been intrigued by the voices, and I gave it to her."

Immediately, He said so clearly, "Angel, didn't I give the radio back to you? I gave it back to you in a different way."

You see, I am now on the radio. I host a radio program every Saturday on WFST at 12:05 p.m., right after the world news in Caribou, Maine, called *Destiny Moments*. During the program, I interview real people with real issues and a real destiny.

Isn't that a neat story?

That is the goodness of the God we serve. God tells us he gives back to us. He restores to us the years the locusts have eaten. Can you believe for what you have lost? Do you believe in providence? Have a little chat with Jesus tonight and listen up. You may be surprised at what He wants to say to you.

> *My sheep hear My voice, and I know them,*
> *and they follow Me.* —John 10:27

CHAPTER THIRTEEN

Wholeness

Jesus has a way of making us whole again. When I was going through a difficulty in my life, and I felt too weak to believe on my own, He always sent me people, His Word, or a blessing.

There was one day when life seemed too overwhelming, and I could not seem to even speak His name. I walked out on my porch, and there was a gift bag containing a teddy bear with a card that read: "Here's a hug for you today from J.C. (Jesus Christ)." I know a person left that on my porch, but I also know Jesus placed bringing that gift to me on their heart. Many times, as I walk the journey called "life," I hug that teddy bear. It has such a special place as a gift from my Heavenly Father. I know today who put the teddy bear on my porch, but it doesn't matter. They were just being obedient to the Lord when they left the bag on my step that day—the day I needed hope. It was a day I will always cherish.

Later, God prompted me to give a teddy bear to a woman with two children who had tried to commit suicide several times. I wrote her a card about the love of Jesus and the hope and future ahead of her. God's plan is awesome, and we all have a destiny. The teddy bear and card ministered to her as only Jesus can do through His Spirit. Isn't it great to know a God who can take a simple teddy bear and minister to a hurting heart? I thank God for that experience, and I pray He will use you and me to bring His heart to the world around us.

We get so caught up in the materialism of this world that we forget we are just passing through. When was the last time you asked Him to use you to bring encouragement to someone who needed a tender touch from the Master's hand? His hand extended—that is what we want to be. We want to be hope for the hopeless, love to the hurting, and His heart to all. Let it be so, dear Jesus, let it be so.

Sometimes, all it takes is a phone call and a word of encouragement to someone in need. Sometimes it takes a hug, a gift, a ride, or a smile. Sometimes it just takes listening to a hurting heart. Other times it means dancing with the heart that was rejoicing (a bit of a challenge for me, as dancing does not flow easily through my body).

I have found that you cannot out-give God. He pours in; you give out. He pours in; you give out. We are His vessels that He uses to touch the world. May we all be so full of Him that we ooze to give out, full to overflowing. We are to bring His Holy Spirit and His comfort to those around us—both those who don't know Him and those who do.

Father, each day, give us assignments. Order our footsteps and anoint us to break the yokes. May the world be a better place because Jesus lives in us. When You walked the earth, You made a difference. Now, we desire, dear Lord, to make a difference as if You were here. You live in us, and we want Your kingdom to come, and Your will be done, here on earth as it is in Heaven. Yes, Lord, yes! Use us today.

Ask Him to commission you. I dare you to step out of your comfort zone and let Him work through you to make a difference in the world around you today.

CHAPTER FOURTEEN

Destiny

I believe every life has a special purpose here on earth. I believe we all have gifts and talents from God, and I believe we need to use the gifts and talents He gave us.

I never dreamt that I would be writing a book. I have been a woman of prayer for many years now, and I know the power of prayer. I remember back in the early '90s, I went to leadership training in Rhode Island with Women's Aglow International. It was there that I had my first vision. We were waiting for Bishop T. D. Jakes to speak when I saw glass doors and water gushing from them, and I was just bringing women to the water. I felt like I was doing nothing and kept asking, "Jesus, don't you want me to put them in the water?"

Jesus replied, "No."

So, I would get the next group of women and bring them to the water. I would bring them, but they had to drink for themselves.

> *". . . but whoever drinks of the water that I shall give him will never thirst. But the water that I shall give him will become in him a fountain of water springing up into everlasting life."* —John 4:14

After the leadership training meeting, two women approached me at different times and asked me to pray for them. I remember this so vividly. I was just a young Christian, and I did not know much about prayer, so I asked if my friends who were more spiritual could pray for them. They both said it was to be me, and they said that to me separately. So, I prayed the best I knew how for each of them individually. That was the beginning of my heart reaching out to the hurting.

Prayer is so simple; just talk to your daddy. I believe the water in my vision represented healing, and only you can receive for yourself. Others can lead, but you must receive for yourself. Drink deep, beautiful people, drink deep.

Over the years, I have read several books on prayer. I love the writing of Stormie Omartian, and I used to lead a women's prayer meeting at a local church. It took place on Thursday evenings. One time, I went to the prayer meeting, and no one came. I remember saying, "Okay, Lord, what are we going to pray about tonight?" I felt led to pray for Atlanta, Georgia. I knew nothing about Atlanta, but I did know how to pray, so I prayed for the people in Atlanta that night. A few weeks went by, and I was home pairing mismatched socks from the mismatched sock bucket, when I came across a Charisma magazine that my then-husband or my children must have tossed into the sock bucket. I opened it right to the "Threshing Floor Conference" at The Dome, in Atlanta, Georgia. My heart began to pound. I felt Him leading me to go to that prayer conference. That night my prayer partner friend called. I shared the connection with her and asked her to pray about it as well. Two weeks later, she called to say she had booked our tickets. I was so excited.

I was even more excited when I learned that Stormie Omartian was going to speak!

I began to ask the Lord for a divine appointment with her. I have been so inspired by her writing, and I just love her honesty and transparency. Sure enough, she had a book signing, and I waited for her to sign mine. I invited her to Maine, and I believe she will be coming someday.

Incredible authors and speakers filled The Dome for that conference—Darlene Bishop, Juanita Bynum, T. D. Jakes, and many others. It was a life-changing experience. I picked up a brochure for His Song Mentoring Institute while I was there. Again I felt my heart skip a beat or two. I brought it home and prayed about it. It seemed like an impossibility, so I threw the brochure away.

Several days later, a friend who had accompanied us to Atlanta brought that same brochure to me. I knew God must have been leading me to go, so I filled the brochure out. Sure enough, my application was selected, and I flew to Tennessee. Judy Jacobs, the mentor at the institute, is an incredible woman of God, and I felt extremely privileged to be mentored by her. Through prayers, teleconferences, and mentoring, she has encouraged me to fulfill my destiny. I knew the Lord was calling me to begin to write, I am fulfilling that part of my destiny with this book. Judy Jacobs has authored books that have helped me stand strong through my trials and reach toward my Promised Land.

I also had the incredible opportunity to attend the Glorieta Writer's Conference in New Mexico where I met so many wonderful people and prayed with so many awesome participants. I joined my faith with women who had several abortions—some who had never walked through healing and some who had. Some of them had friends who had up to twelve abortions; others only had one. I knew that the Lord wanted to use this particular healing in my life and in my writings. I had never been so sure of anything.

On my flight home, I sat beside an executive of a large corporation. I should have missed that plane after arriving an hour and ten minutes late to Cincinnati from Albuquerque. I sat in my friend's seat, as she had sat in mine. The woman beside me looked at me and said, "I cannot believe that they held this plane for you."

We began to converse, and before I knew it, she was confessing her abortion to me. This sort of confession also happened in New Mexico, and it occurs in Maine regularly. I believe the Lord held the plane for her that night, not me. She no longer will hold the secret shame of abortion in her heart.

I never thought I would write about abortion; it is a very controversial and emotional subject. But I know I am supposed to share my story and journey of inner healing, in hopes that it will impact the lives of others. And I know God has called me to write and speak about the trauma of abortion.

What are your talents and gifts? We all have them.

Let me repeat myself: we all have them.

Are you using them? Are you not sure what they are? Ask your Heavenly Father; He will show you. He will send others to help—to confirm whatever you need. He is a good God. He loves you. Are you praying for His perfect will? Submit everything you do to Him, and He will direct you.

Man makes his plans, but God orders our footsteps. Reflect on your life and see if you can identify any divine appointments or God encounters. I know you have had them because His Word does not lie. His love for me made me whole and orders my footsteps. Now I pray the same for you.

Destiny awaits, my friend. Destiny is waiting on you.

Ashes No More

~~~~~~

Jesus, Lover of My Soul, Creator of my image, Lifter of my head
My name is Beautiful.
Woman, pure, holy, undefiled. Sanctified, set apart, journeying with Jesus.
A path, narrow and straight, ashes no more.
Trusting her master, her maker, the lover of her soul.
Skipping on the journey with childlike faith, believing her Father knows what's best.
The morning dew, the night's crisp air, reminds her of the kisses from above.
Jesus, the ultimate man, the lover of her soul.
Beautiful, a receiver of His glory, ashes no more.

~~~~~~

Tell Them...

Tell them I love them . . . Tell them they are mine . . .
Tell them I will never leave them nor forsake them.
Tell them they are precious gems . . . Tell them I see
them as perfect.
Tell them they reflect my image . . . Tell them not to
look back.
Tell them to look straight ahead . . . Tell them I laid
out the red carpet for them.
My blood, it was enough.
Tell them, tell them, tell them again!

For God so loved the world that He gave His
only begotten Son, that whoever believes in
Him should not perish but have everlasting
life. —John 3:16

The earth is the Lord's, and all its fullness,
The world and those who dwell therein. For
He has founded it upon the seas, And estab-
lished it upon the waters. Who may ascend
into the hill of the Lord? Or who may stand
in His holy place? He who has clean hands
and a pure heart, Who has not lifted up his
soul to an idol, Nor sworn deceitfully. He
shall receive blessing from the Lord, And

righteousness from the God of his salvation. This is Jacob, the generation of those who seek Him, Who seek Your face. Selah Lift up your heads, O you gates! And be lifted up, you everlasting doors! And the King of glory shall come in. Who is this King of glory? The Lord strong and mighty, The Lord mighty in battle. Lift up your heads, O you gates! Lift up, you everlasting doors! And the King of glory shall come in. Who is this King of glory? The Lord of hosts, He is the King of glory. Selah. —Psalm 24

Recovered Well

You are amazing. You were created in the image of a great God, and He has a great destiny for your life. It is such a blessing to journey life with Jesus Christ and one another.

My prayer for you, now that you are on the journey toward healing, is that you will help others in their healing processes. The words of the Apostle John are so true:

Therefore, if the Son makes you free, you shall be free indeed. —John 8:36

Live free, laugh often, love deeply, beautiful people, and turn the world upside down for God's glory. He is so worthy of your devotion. I want to end my recovery story with this: to all the beautiful people of the world, I write these words for you, from the heart of a Heavenly Father in love with all His beautiful people.

About the Author

Angel L. Murchison shares her journey of overcoming the trauma of abortion and seeks to bring women to the cleansing grace of Jesus Christ. Angel is the founder of Healing Waters Women's Ministry, the author of *Good Morning Beautiful People: Angel's Prayer of the Day,* and a radio talk show host on *Destiny Moments* where she interviews real people with real issues and a real destiny. She resides in Presque Isle, Maine and is the mother of three adult daughters and eight beautiful grandchildren.

Angel's Bible Study on Abortion

If you have had one abortion or several abortions, I want you to know that God is not mad at you. Jesus died for all our sins. He loves you; He truly loves you!

I want you to journey with me for the next three days. On the first day, we are going to address the hurt—the pain carried inside that Jesus can, and will, heal. We are going to invite the Holy Spirit in and ask Him to help us on this path and help us remember what we need to know. Then we are going to ask him to heal us.

Journal everything on this journey. Make it as deep and personal as you want. This is your walk with your Creator. You were created in His image, and your aborted child(ren) were as well.

Let's Pray

Father, here we are in your Holy presence with a void that needs to be filled. We need to be made whole again. Father, I realize it is only You who can take away all the inner pain, hurts, and turmoil and bring peace, love, and joy. Father, I pray for you to restore my life and make me whole again. Amen.

DAY 1: I AM HURT

Today, I have chosen to face that I made a wrong choice and acknowledge that every life has purpose.

Let's look at and write out the following scriptures:

Jeremiah 1:4–5

_____

_____

_____

_____

Psalm 139:13–16

_____

_____

_____

_____

What were your thoughts and feelings when you first became aware that you were pregnant?

_____

_____

_____

_____

Can you identify the reason you terminated the pregnancy? Can you recall the details of the abortion procedure? (town, city, state, doctor's office, clinic, people in the room, who drove you, etc.)

_____

_____

_____

_____

What were your feelings after the abortion?

_____

_____

_____

_____

What are you experiencing today from the choice to have an abortion?

_____

_____

_____

_____

How do you think the decision to have an abortion has changed you?

_____

_____

_____

_____

Do you believe the scripture in John 8:36? (Write it out)

_____

_____

_____

_____

Can you receive the freedom Jesus died for in regard to your abortion?

_____

_____

_____

_____

Notes and Prayer:

_____

_____

_____

_____

Day 2: The Grieving Process

Have you ever grieved the loss of your child? Do you know whether your baby was a boy or girl?

_____

_____

_____

_____

Have you named your child? If yes, write out your child's name. If no, do you want to name your child? (This doesn't have to be done today, but pray about naming your child. God will help you.)

_____

_____

_____

_____

Your baby is in Heaven. Do you believe this? Write out scriptures to support this.

_____

_____

_____

_____

What emotions are you feeling now? Can you write them out?

_____

_____

_____

_____

Can you forgive the person(s) involved? Can you forgive yourself?

_____

_____

_____

_____

List the people you need to forgive.

_____

_____

_____

_____

Let's look at some scriptures on forgiveness:

Psalm 103:3

_____

_____

_____

_____

Psalm 65:3

_____

_____

_____

_____

Psalm 32:5

_____

_____

_____

_____

1 John 1:9

_____

_____

_____

_____

Luke 7:36

_____

_____

_____

_____

Let's write some letters of forgiveness. Take your time and be specific as you write each letter. No one will see them but you, and you

can destroy them or keep them. This is your personal journey to freedom. This may take you longer, according to the list of people you have to forgive. Every letter you write and release to God is well worth the time.

Write a letter to your child. What do you want to say? What is important for your child to know? Ask the Holy Spirit to help you express your feelings, buried emotions, etc. in this letter to your precious child. You can be assured your baby girl or baby boy is in the arms of Jesus and loves you beyond anything that can be measured.

DAY 3: A DAY OF REMEMBRANCE

Today, we want to focus on the life of our child. He or she is in Heaven now. Jesus is the best Father, the best parent. Do you believe this?

_____

_____

_____

_____

Are you ready to release the pain of the past and receive the healing that Christ paid for?

_____

_____

_____

_____

We have been forgiven. We no longer need to carry guilt and shame. Write out the following verses.

Psalm 34:4–5

_____

_____

_____

_____

Isaiah 54:4–8

_____

_____

_____

_____

Psalm 126:5

_____

_____

_____

_____

Are you ready to have a remembrance? Today we will put together a small remembrance of our child's life.

Let's take the letter we wrote earlier and write words on some petals. I use fake white petals I purchased at a craft store, and I put the petals in a baby pouch with my letter. Some of my words included precious and loved. Be creative. You can plant a flower, plant a tree, or purchase something to put inside your home in remembrance of your baby. One thing that's for sure is that God will help you find the perfect remembrance. He helped me find the Precious Moments boy in the Christian bookstore, and He will help you find something equally unique and special. I have that figurine and my letter with seven white petals in a small pouch in my china closet. I smile big when my eyes catch a glimpse of it, and I remember my son.

Thank You

Thank you for taking this journey with me. Please feel free to reach out to your local Pregnancy Care Center if you need immediate help. If you would like to contact me or my ministry, please search for Healing Waters Women's Ministry, P.O. Box 1177, Presque Isle, Maine 04769. You can also email me at amurchison07@gmail.com.

If you have enjoyed my life story and would like to journey with me in daily prayer, please check out my other books: *Good Morning Beautiful People, Angel's Prayer of The Day*. These daily devotionals are full of life experiences, rich in the Word of God, and will cause you to hunger and thirst for more of Him. You will soon discover He truly is Emmanuel, God with us.

I am available to speak at conferences, healing retreat weekends, and churches, as well as being available for personal, one-on-one ministry via phone, Zoom, or other means of communication.

The best is yet to come, my friend.

A free ebook edition is available with the purchase of this book.

To claim your free ebook edition:

1. Visit MorganJamesBOGO.com
2. Sign your name CLEARLY in the space
3. Complete the form and submit a photo of the entire copyright page
4. You or your friend can download the ebook to your preferred device

(M·J) Morgan James BOGO™

A **FREE** ebook edition is available for you or a friend with the purchase of this print book.

CLEARLY SIGN YOUR NAME ABOVE

Instructions to claim your free ebook edition:
1. Visit MorganJamesBOGO.com
2. Sign your name CLEARLY in the space above
3. Complete the form and submit a photo of this entire page
4. You or your friend can download the ebook to your preferred device

Print & Digital Together Forever.

Snap a photo   Free ebook   Read anywhere